Welcome to the Art of Kumomi™

A meditative art medium embracing originality in a freeform style.

Seeing an image or feeling an emotion in color and expressing it through the paint brush and bold inks. A form that appears *out of the Clouds*.

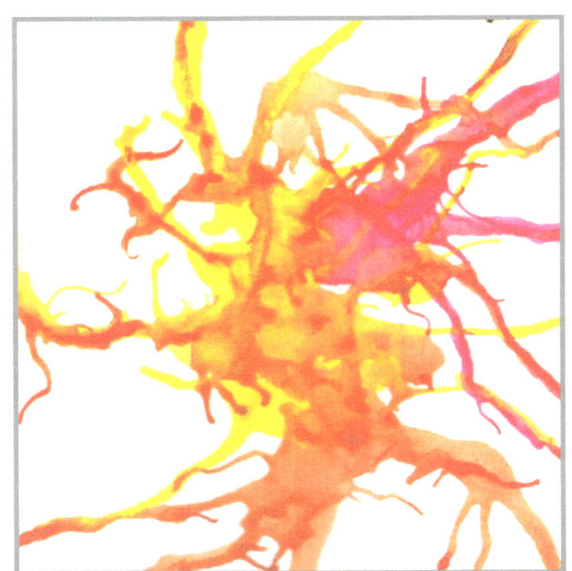 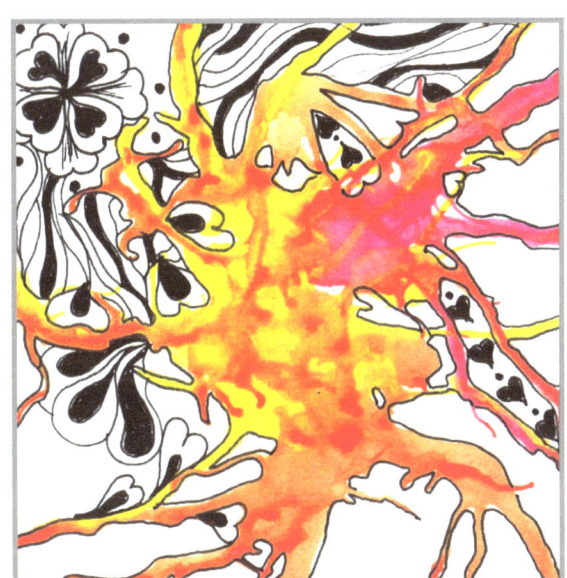

OUT of the CLOUD

by

ALISANN SMOOKLER, Fine Artist

All Rights Reserved© 2023 Art by Alisann

I wish you hope and calm.
Let calm embrace you and hope fill your heart.
—Alisann

INTRODUCTION

I believe that art is healing. Throughout my life when I would move away from creating art, a life event would bring me back to my art. In 2013 I was diagnosed with terminal brain cancer. The doctors told me I had two months to live. After brain surgery and radiation I began my healing. My focus was to exercise my brain by drawing and painting each and every day. It is now 2023 and I am 10 years cancer free. My art has given me a way to reduce stress, build my confidence and support me through my healing journey.

In late 2017 I saw a flyer for an art class at my local art supply store. It was titled *The Art of Kumomi*™ *Finding Meaning in Randomness*. It caught my attention and I was immediately intrigued. I signed up for the class.

In the workshop I found a new way to express myself and add to my art healing modalities. What I love most is the core essence of the process which is mediation and calm. We all need to take time in our lives to stop, be open and vulnerable to support ourselves in the spirit of love, peace and well-being. The art of Kumomi™ gives us that opportunity. It is truly an art form which comes from ones ability to simply let go! You do not have to have any artistic skill to create the art of Kumomi™. It's not about perfection or correctness.

It is about the process and how you feel as you create the art.

The definition of Kumomi - *Cloud Watching*

This art technique was created by Karen Elaine-Artist, Author, Designer

It is easier to fall down and give up.
The reward for not falling down initiates a surrender that opens the heart to hope.
-Alisann

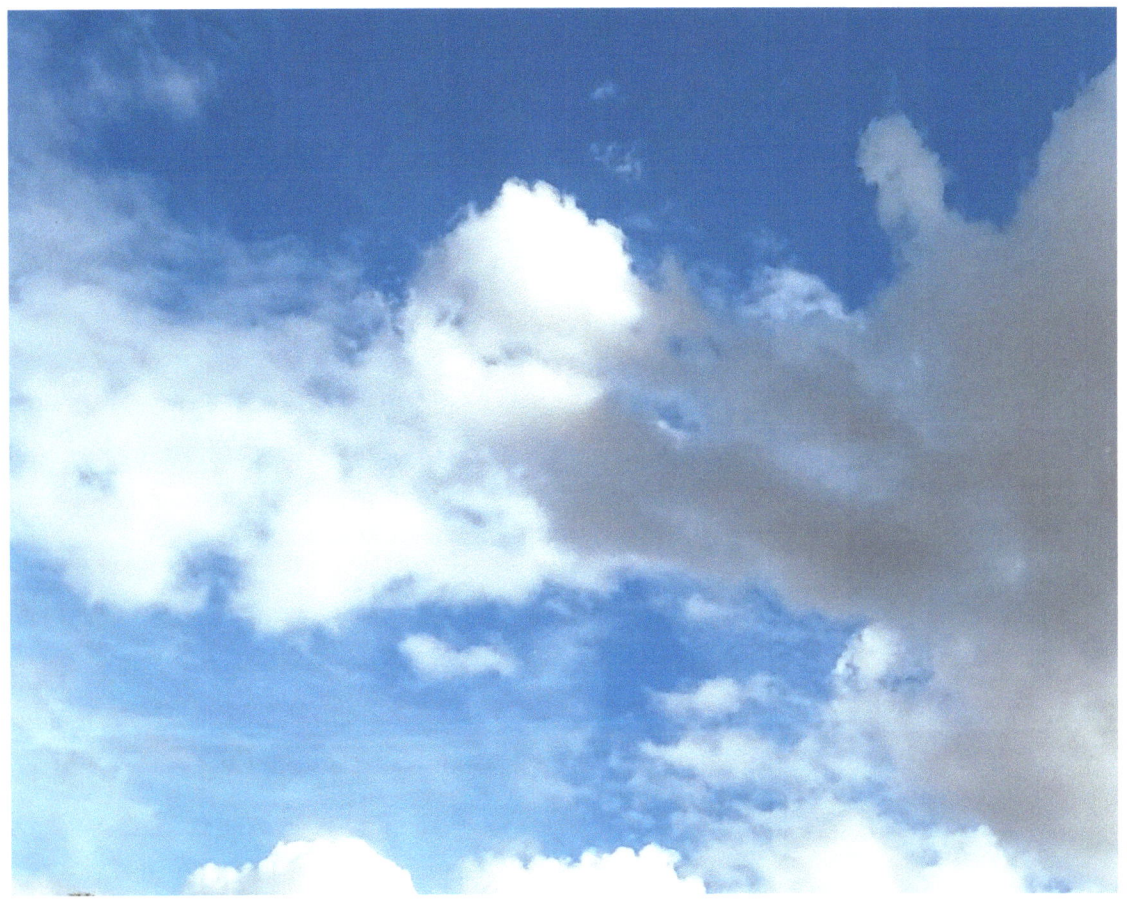

You are probably asking "what does cloud watching have to do with painting?" In the art of Kumomi™ as you paint, what you "see" in your painting is exactly the same as cloud watching.

What do you see in this cloud photo of the sky?

I see a large hand reaching out from the right as its' finger tips touch a beautiful white carnation. You might see something entirely different.

This is the randomness in the creative art form of Kumomi™

What I have learned about hope...it is always present.
As long as I focus on hope; it is my foundation.
-Alisann

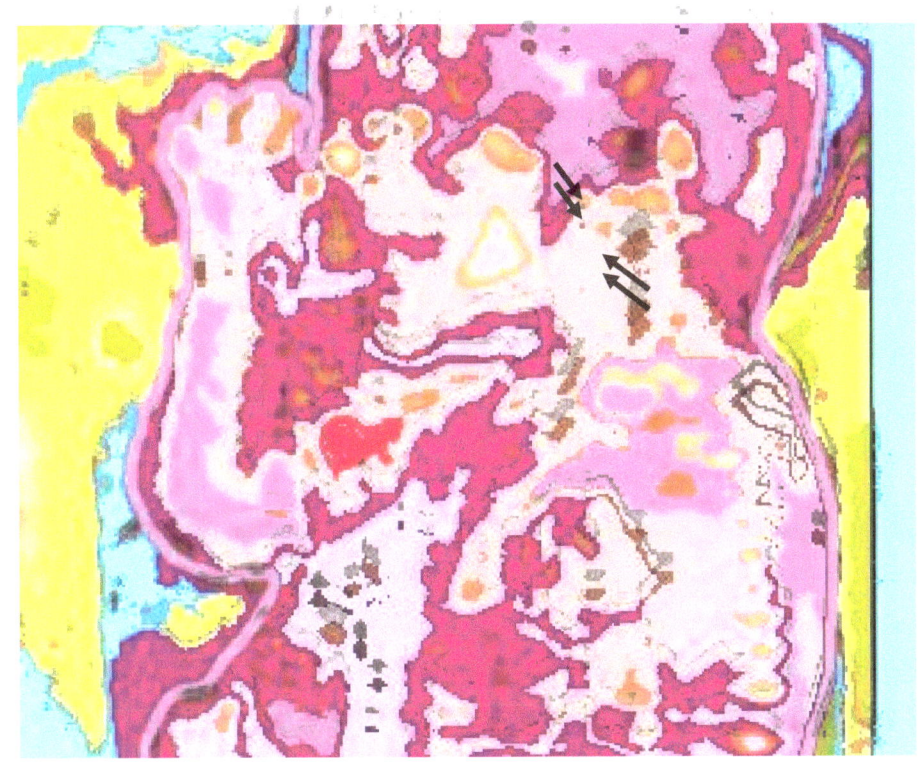

Here is an example of finding randomness in another art form. This is Baby Ultrasound art. In 90% of the ultrasounds I paint, I find heart shapes somewhere in the echo bands of the ultrasound. In this artwork I enhanced the heart shape that appeared in the ultrasound.

TIME TO LET GO

Creating the Art of Kumomi™ is a time to let go, be open to whatever appears and then move into a more focused mindset to finalize the art with doodles. While I love the free form part of this process, my favorite part is the doodling. My mind is in a constant state of movement due to the post-effects of my brain surgery and radiation treatments. When I doodle, it allows my mind to stop and focus directly on the doodling process. Once my mind is focused all the feeling of movement stops and my mind is stable and calm.

It is the **intention on focus** that brings you to **calm and serenity**.

No matter the challenge, I can face it head on with
HOPE
-Alisann

CREATING YOUR SPACE TO PAINT

Very little space is needed. Perhaps a table on the patio, your kitchen table, or anywhere you can set up a quiet workspace that has plenty of light, a flat surface and a comfortable chair. Place a waterproof material on the table in case of ink/water splashes. (I use a plastic trash bag)

Keep your feet flat on the floor to be grounded.

The essence of this art form is to have a meditative experience. I personally play meditation music while painting. When the painting is drying, I do a 20-30 minute meditation before starting the doodles. It is important that the inks are fully dry before beginning the doodling process.

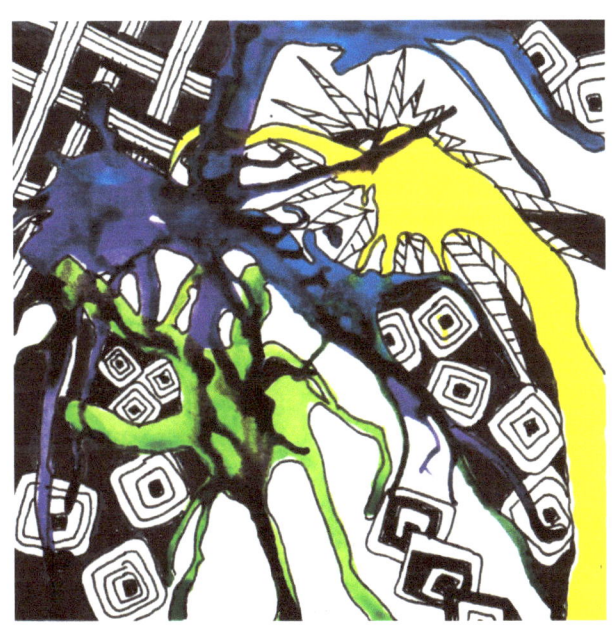
BUCKET FULL OF SUNSHINE

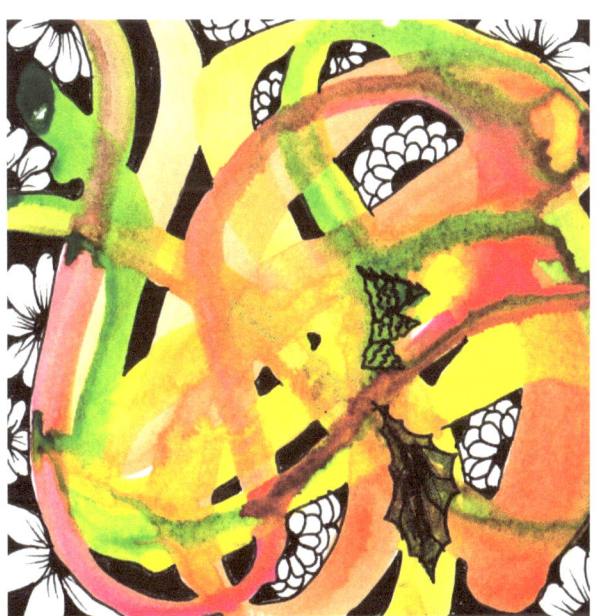
FALL

If we do not have hope; then what do we have?
-Alisann

CREATIVE TOOLS/SUPPLIES

INKS

I use Golden High Flow Acrylics. Colors: Quinacridone Magenta, Phthalo Blue Red Shade, Hansa Yellow Light. (You can use any colors you like, but these mix well to produce other colors.) This is where a Color Wheel helps. Watercolors can also be used, but will not have the same intensity of color as the inks.

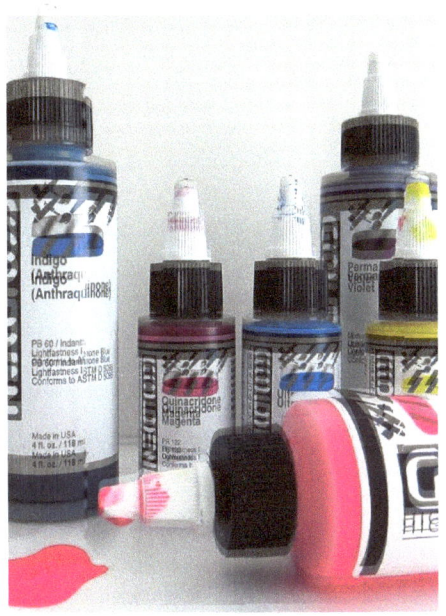

PALETTE

6 petal/well plastic paint palette.

A bowl for water.

BRUSHES

Soft brushes are best. No need to purchase expensive brushes. Round and Filbert.

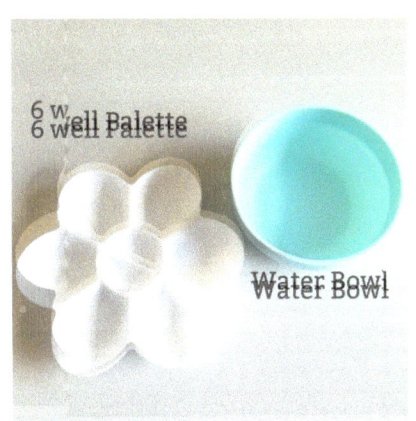

PENS

Black felt-tip pens in assorted sizes. Be sure they are waterproof.

ART APRON

Protect your clothing when painting.

Supplies can be purchased on Amazon or any art store.

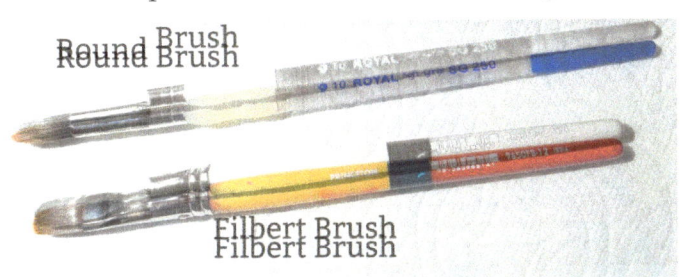

Round Brush

Filbert Brush

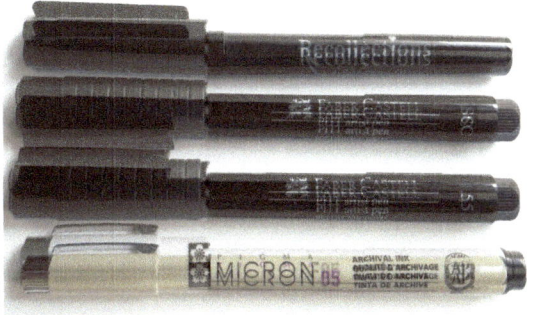

Wake up with Gratitude and watch how your day evolves.
-Alisann

Choose your painting surface: Gesso Board or watercolor paper tile. You need a substrate that is not too absorbent. The paint should blend well with the other colors, but not soak in quickly as that can create "muddy" colors.

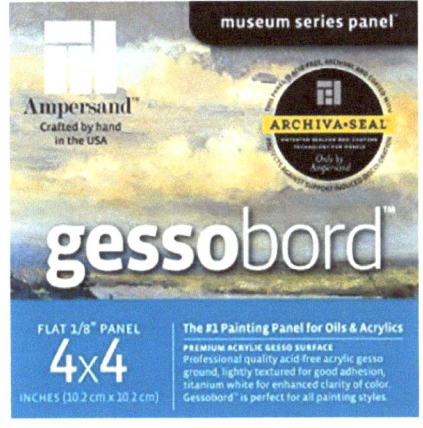
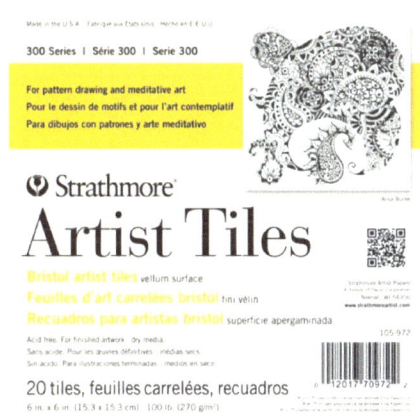

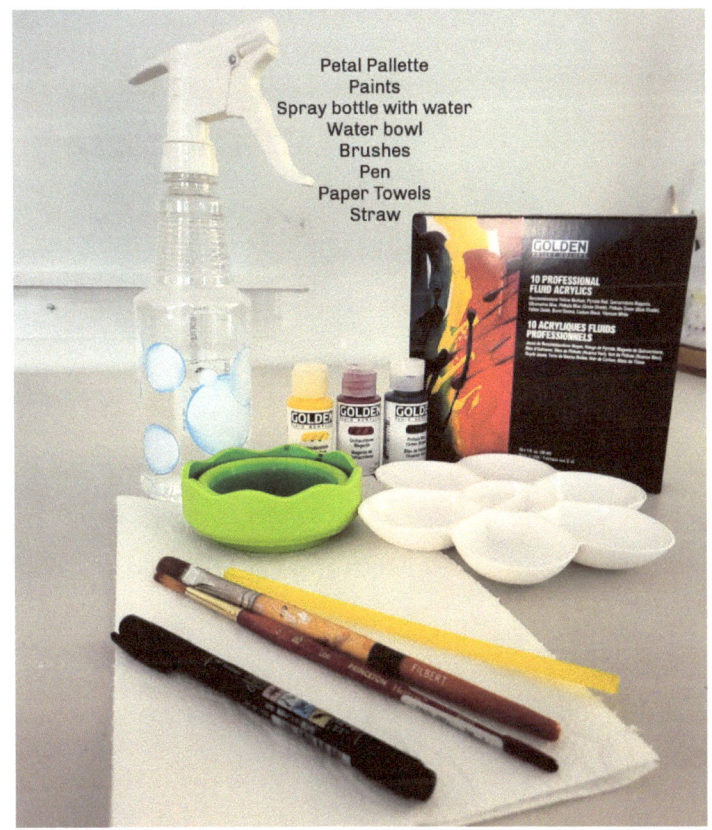

Petal Pallette
Paints
Spray bottle with water
Water bowl
Brushes
Pen
Paper Towels
Straw

Having hope means never feeling alone.
-Alisann

BEGIN THE PROCESS

Once you have set up your tools, sit down, *stop*, take a deep breath and set your intention. I start my music, close my eyes, *state* my intention, and then begin by taking the inks and putting several drops of each color in the palette. Mix the colors to create 3 more additional colors on your palette. Use a color wheel for mixing colors if you need to. Have plenty of water in your bowl as the inks are very concentrated and water is a key element in the process.

Take your time as you mix the colors. Everything we do in creating Kumomi™ is done mindfully. We don't want to rush through the process as it is important to focus our intention on the simplicity of the process.

Take your brush and choose a color to begin. There are two ways to approach the painting: abstract, with no specific form, or have a word (mantra) in your mind. For the word approach, you can paint the word in a very abstract style. Clean your brush in the water grabbing another color with each stroke or letter of a word.

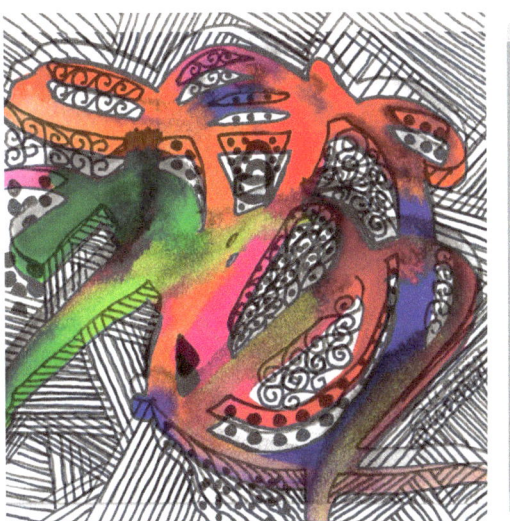

When painting this tile I painted the letters for LOVE. Stacking letter on letter creates an abstract effect. You can see how each letter is a different color and how they merged together to form other colors.

When you reach out and offer your support, you are giving Hope.
-Alisann

INTENTION - FREEFORM STYLE

Choosing a word or simply letting the paint flow onto the tile, allow your **mindfulness** to guide you. Paint in broad strokes with your arm and wrist while sweeping strokes in letters or randomness. Hold the brush gently, not tightly with your fingertips. Be liberal with the water on your brush. Leave white areas and do not completely cover the tile in color. They can be left white or doodles added to complete your art piece. It is your creation. You will know when to stop painting and if you want to add doodles or not.

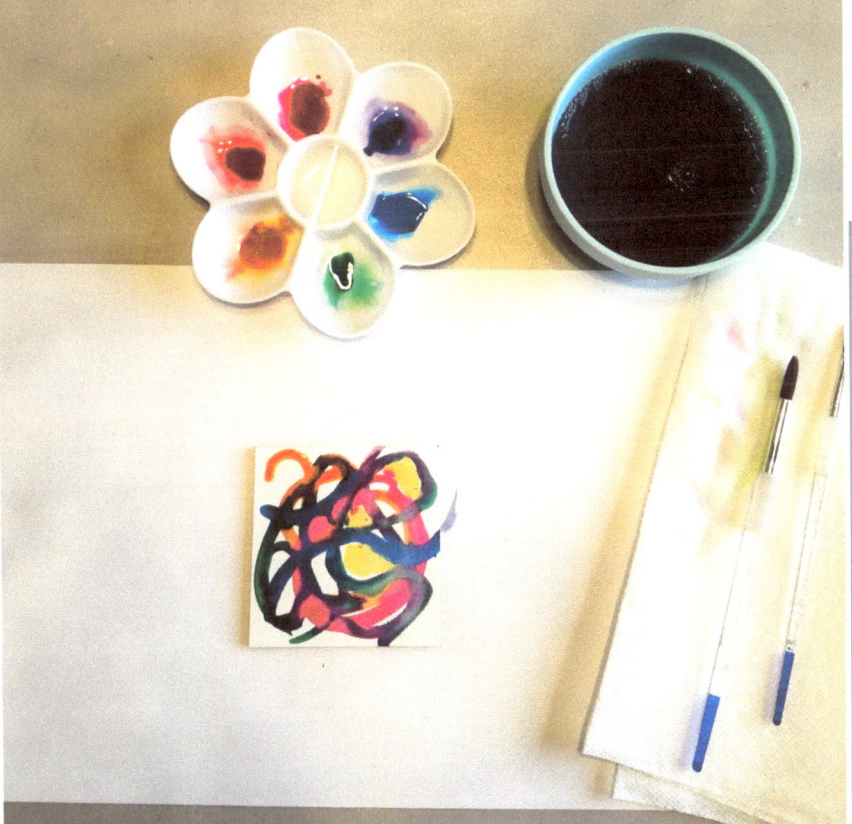

My preference is to add the Doodles as they bring a bold dimension/contrast to the art.

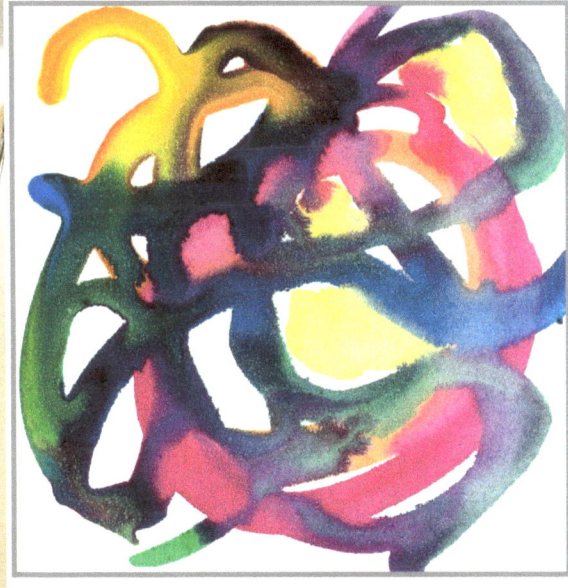

I painted the letters SOUL on top of each other to create this tile.

Each day brings a new hurdle to climb. You cannot go around it. You must climb over it to see hope on the other side.
 -Alisann

OUTLINE YOUR PAINTING

When your tile is completely dry move to the next step. Take your dry tile and a black waterproof felt-tip pen (fine point), begin to outline the painted design. Outline each white area of your design. Even the smallest ones as you see in the example below.

Relax and let go. As you outline the design open your imagination and notice any shapes or forms that pop out. You may not see any and that is okay.

There are no rules in Kumomi™. There is no right or wrong...there JUST IS!

You will begin to feel the free flow of creativity.

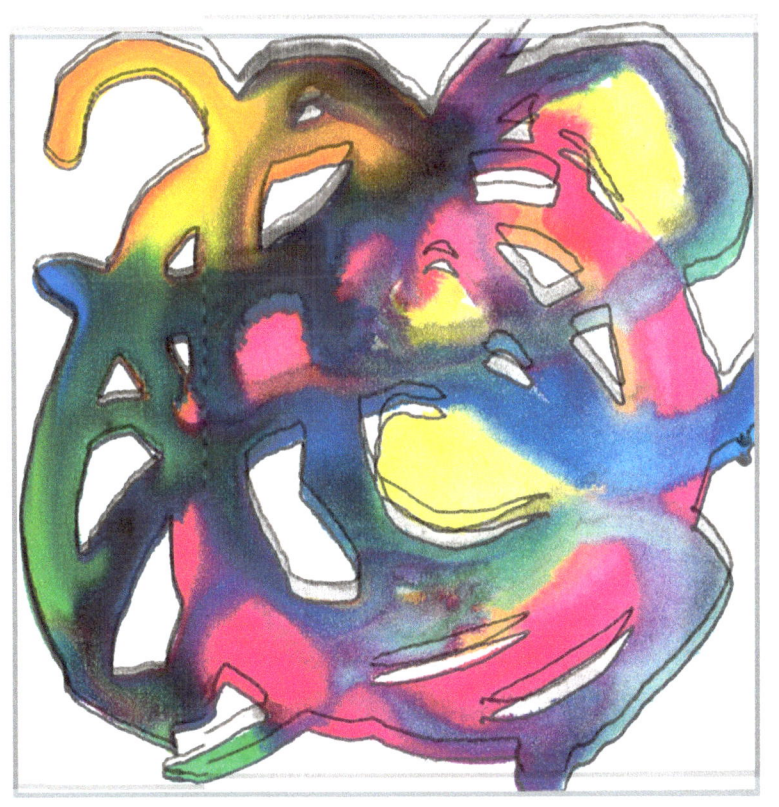

SUGGESTION

As the tile is drying do a 30 minute Meditation or Yoga session. It will keep you in that calm open state as you continue to create your art with doodles.

The only obstacle standing in my way is me!
-Alisann

MINDFUL DOODLES

The tile is now ready to add the Doodles. As a coloring book artist I have become very fond of Doodles. They allow you to freestyle draw without drawing a perfect line. Creating patterns of black and white areas that enhance the art. Practice drawing on a blank sheet of paper if you are new to doodling. The doodles will complete your art work and add another dimension to the piece. As you begin to add your doodles to the painted tile, begin the *Cloud Watching* exercise to find those random shapes and objects. Hearts, flowers, bubbles. Adding dots, dashes, lines. circles.......anything you want! My Doodles below.

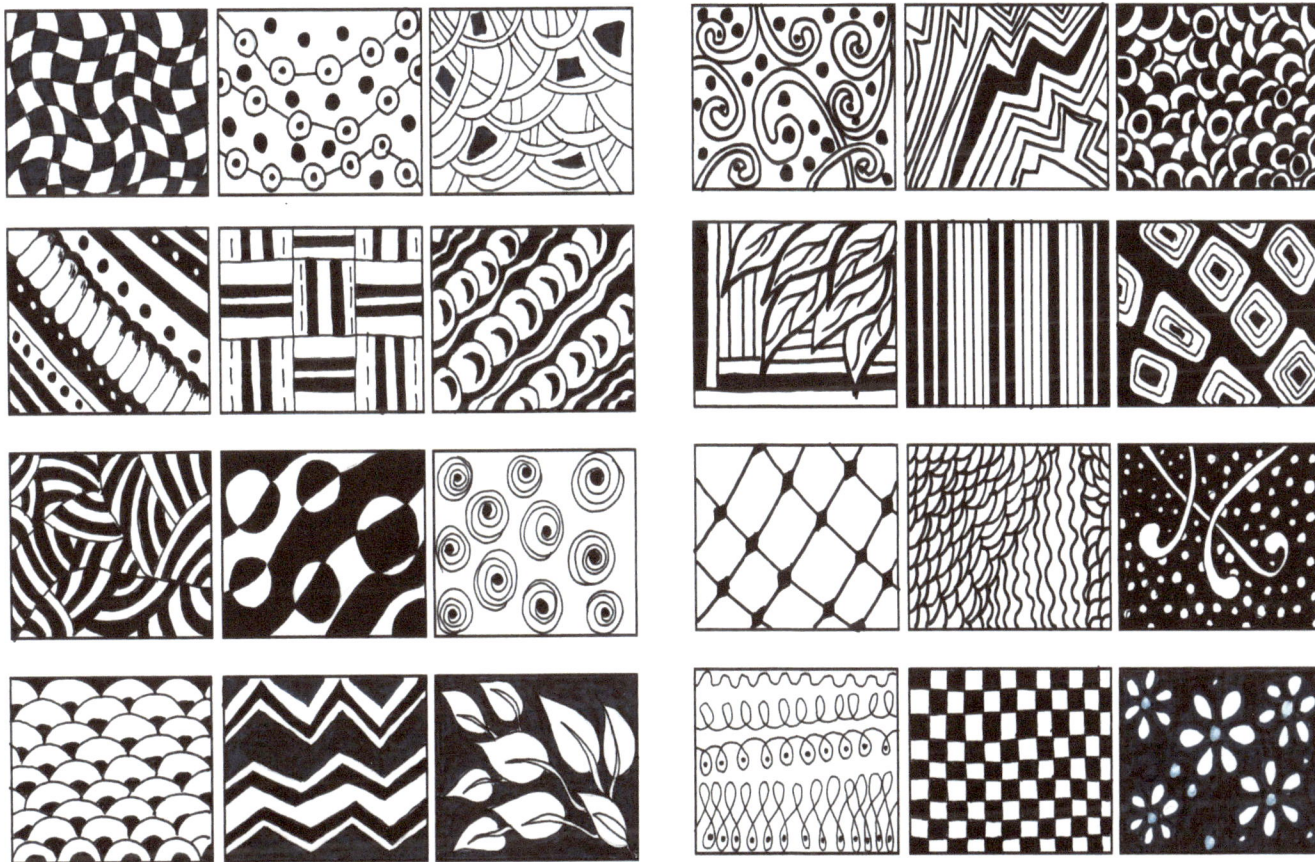

It's not enough to "just" hope. It begins by placing one foot in front of the other. The seed of hope is then planted and will begin to grow.
-Alisann

Draw each line, curve or loop mindfully with intention. Keep a balance of black and white to further enhance the art. You will know when it is done. It is **YOUR MINDFUL ART**.

You may choose to apply an Acrylic spray Varnish to protect it as the last step.

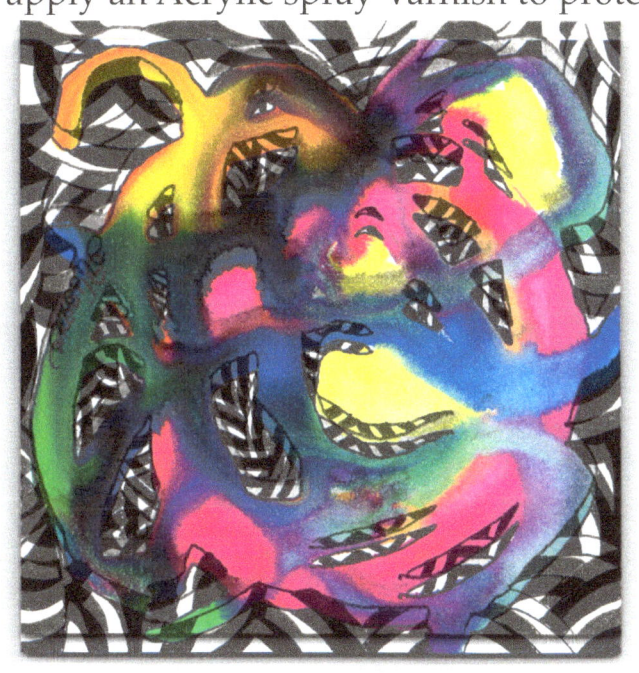

Once your artwork is complete, be sure to sign your work. This is your creation and your work of art. Honor yourself with your signature. This came from inside your heart and soul. Take that moment, as one does at the end of a yoga session, and say NAMASTE'

There is no better way to honor yourself and your spirit than creating art. It requires you to be vulnerable and be open to all that is healing and supportive. My healing journey would probably have a much different outcome if I was not able to open my mind, body and spirit to **ART**.

When we wish things could have been different, we cannot change the past. When we hope for a better today, we begin the process of change.
-Alisann

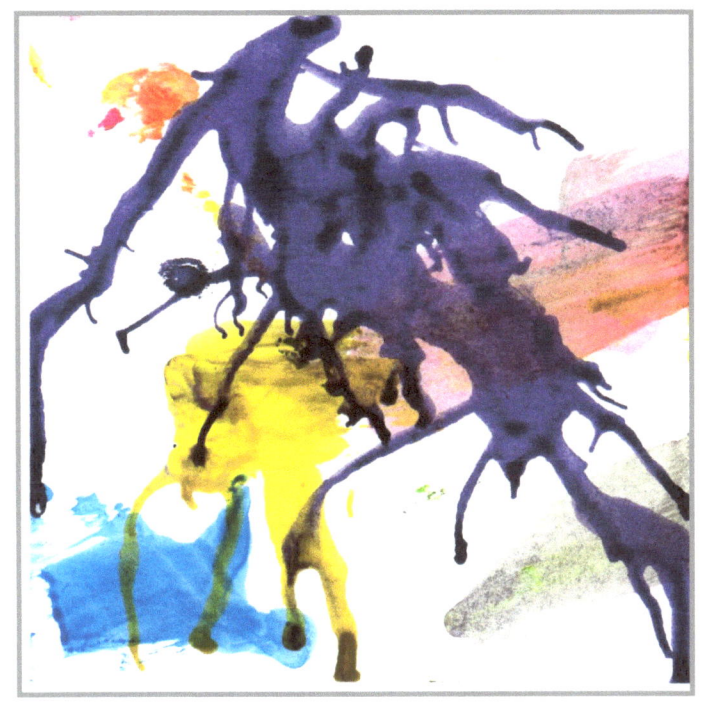

BEFORE DOODLES — AFTER DOODLES

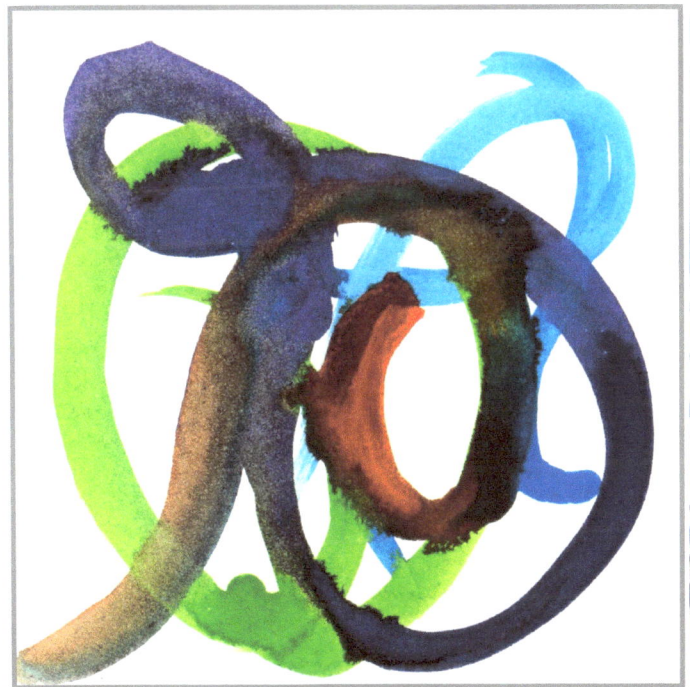
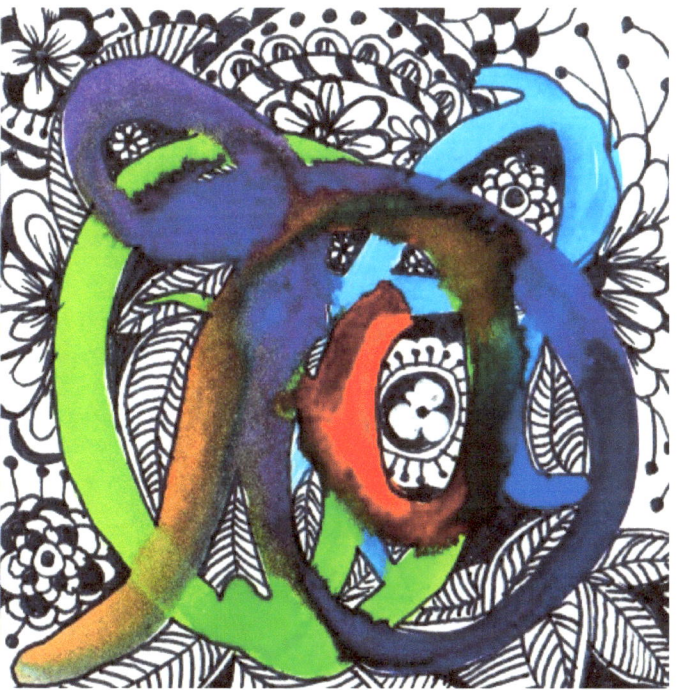

I can see beyond the horizon and hope is rising with the sun!
-Alisann

THE GIFT OF ART

Kumomi™ is an art form for all ages, and abilities. Sharing in a group setting can be calming, joyful and rewarding. Watching others create and then sharing your artwork with others in the group is empowering.

Or having quiet time to yourself to create. There is no judgement in this art form. It's an expression of LOVE to ones' SELF.

Take that time and space to honor yourself.

In 2014 I began sharing Kumomi™ and my coloring books in Cancer support groups. It's an honor to guide these groups through an art experience. When attendees walk into the support group with sad or troubled expressions, after a short period of time I see them change. They forget their illness or their tough day and smiles appear. They walk out with a beautiful sense of calm. Most importantly they have taken time for themselves.

An important element in the healing process.

MORE IDEAS WITH KUMOMI™

- Use Glitter, White, and Metallic pens along with Black
- Try different sizes of tiles
- Create a Journal with your painted tiles
- Create Greeting Cards, Gift Tags
- Frame your art
- Create and Affirmation book

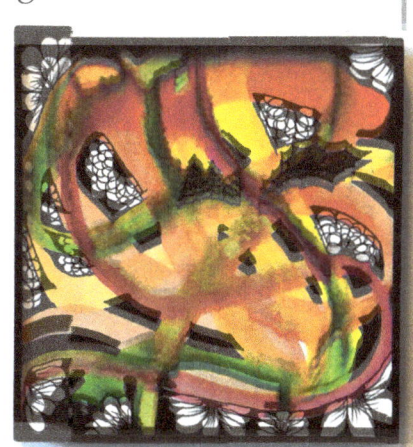

Hope can be fleeting if you lose focus.
-Alisann

OVERVIEW Step by Step

Collect your supplies then sit down in a comfortable chair stating your intention.

Turn on music and open your mind to randomness.

Relax as you paint in a loose open style. Be Spontaneous. Options -Use a straw to lightly blow on the wet inks to create more patterns. Use a spray bottle, lightly spraying the inks while they are wet for more movement in your art piece.

Focus on your intention.

When doodling, draw each stroke slowly and deliberately.

After the outline is completed, look in-between the colors for shapes and forms. If you do not see anything rotate the tile. Or close your eyes for a few minutes opening them to look again at the tile.

Don't force the experience.

This entire experience is a *MINDFUL* one.
There is no right or wrong way.
No judgement or self-criticism.

Sign your art when complete.

Write the date and your feelings on the back of your tile.

Enjoy the Experience !

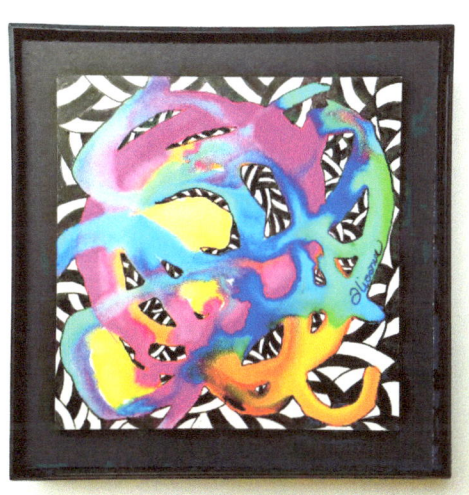

CELEBRATION

Hope is waiting just behind that obstacle.
-Alisann

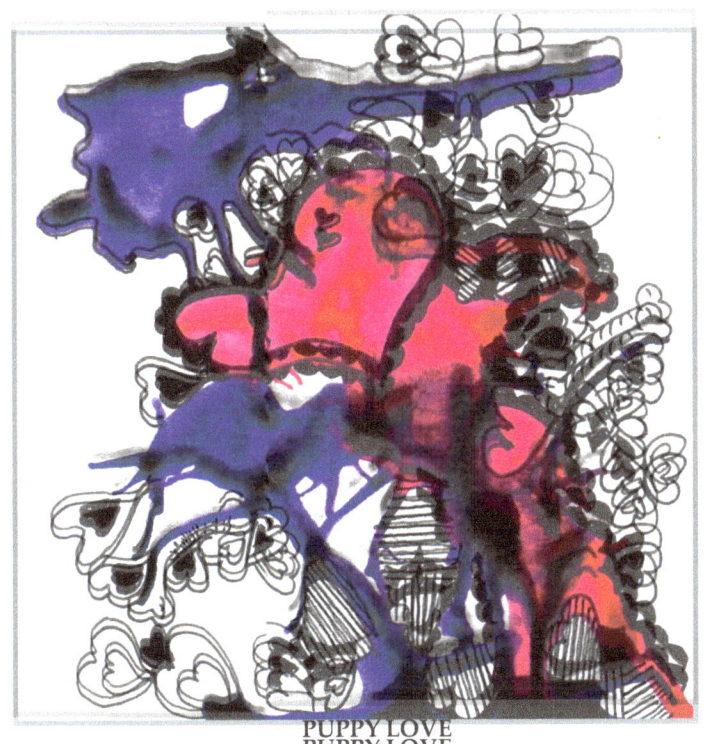

PUPPY LOVE

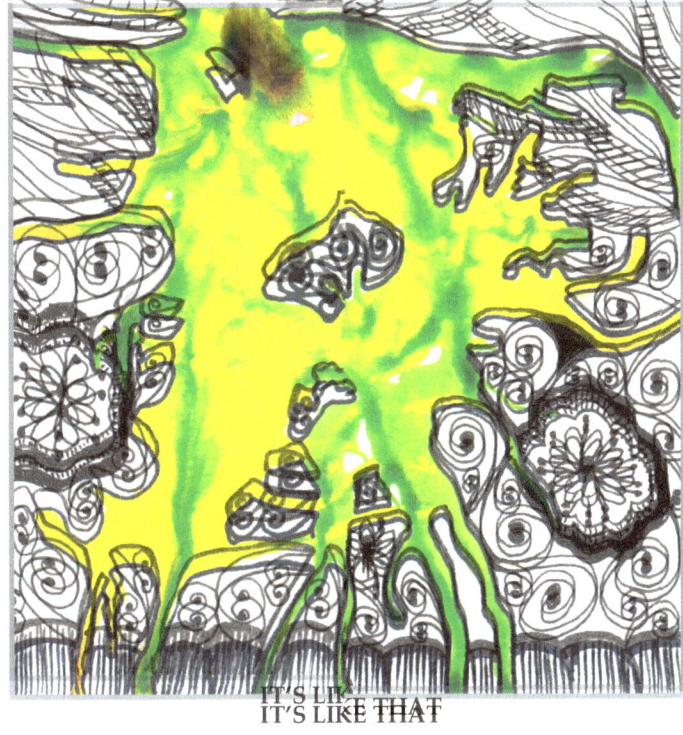

IT'S LIKE THAT

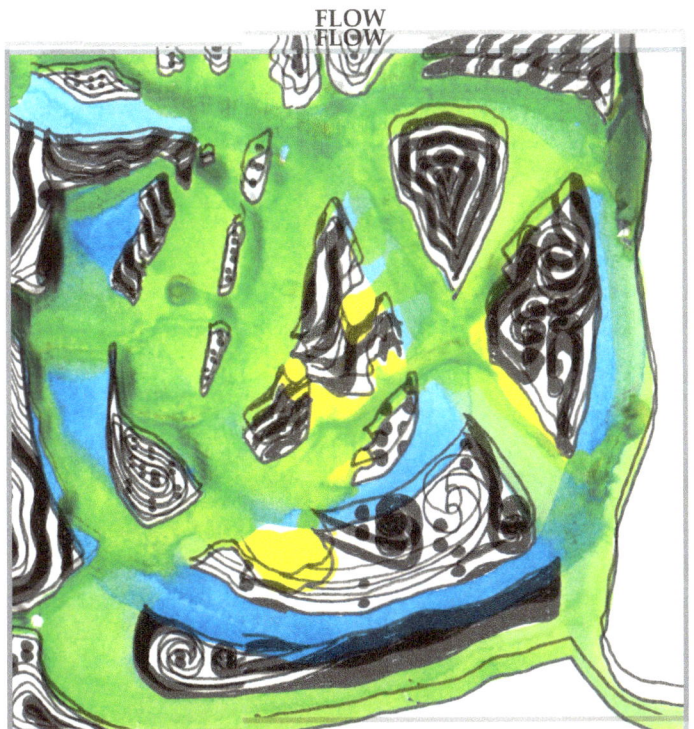

FLOW

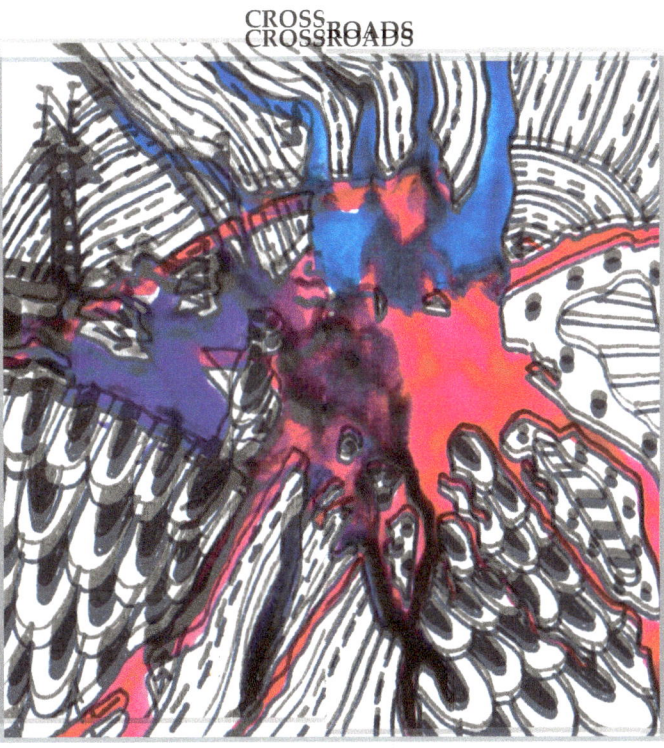

CROSSROADS

There is nothing more profound than when that "aha" moment occurs and hope is realized!
-Alisann

WHERE TO PURCHASE SUPPLIES

Most of the supplies I found on Amazon and at my local Art Supply store.

Artist Tiles—Gesso tiles/Ampersand (Brand)

Pens—Black Pens: Micron (Brand), Farber-Castell PITT, Multiliner (Be sure they are Waterproof) White Pen: Molotow

Brushes—Craft stores (Any brand that is a round brush) Michaels carries a brand called Artist Loft that is very affordable

Palette—Yasutomo (Brand) or any petal palette at art stores or Amazon

Golden High Flow Acrylics—Amazon or any art store goldenpaints.com

Acrylic Varnish—Satin—Brands/Golden, Liquitex

Frames—Michaels Crafts—Brand/Studio Décor

These frames from Michaels are inexpensive and they can sit on a table or hang on a wall. They come with glass and in multiple sizes. My paper tiles, I mount under the glass. My gesso tiles, I mount without the glass.

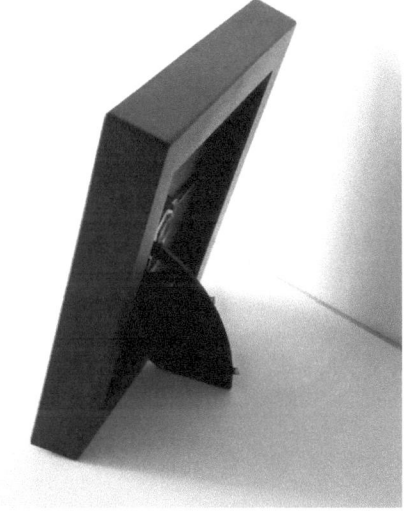
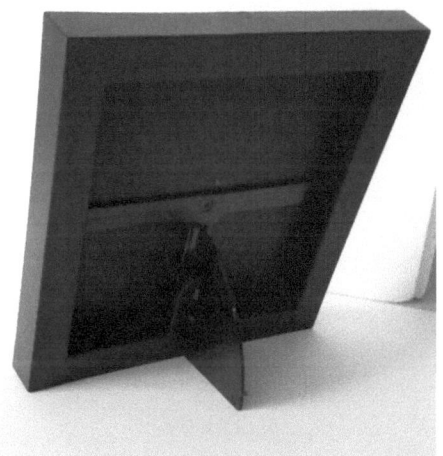

It's unlikely you will find hope in fear.
You will find hope in your heart!
-Alisann

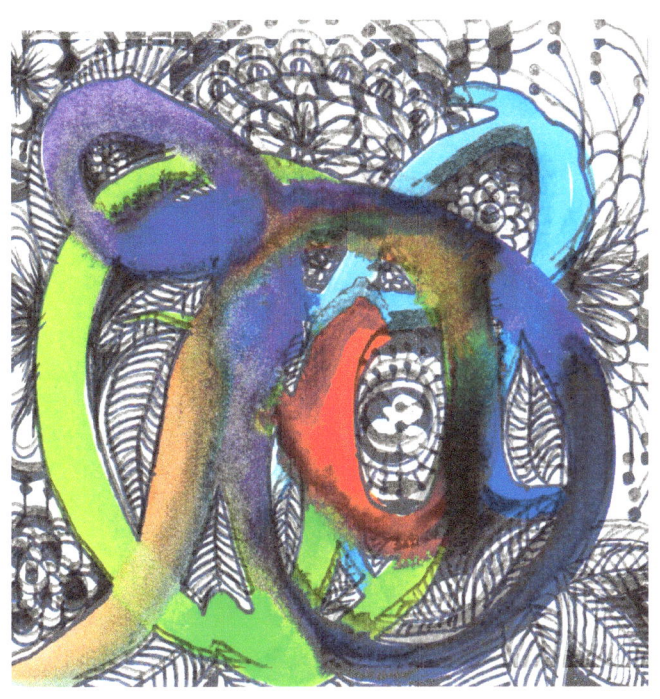

SPRING

LEAP OF FAITH

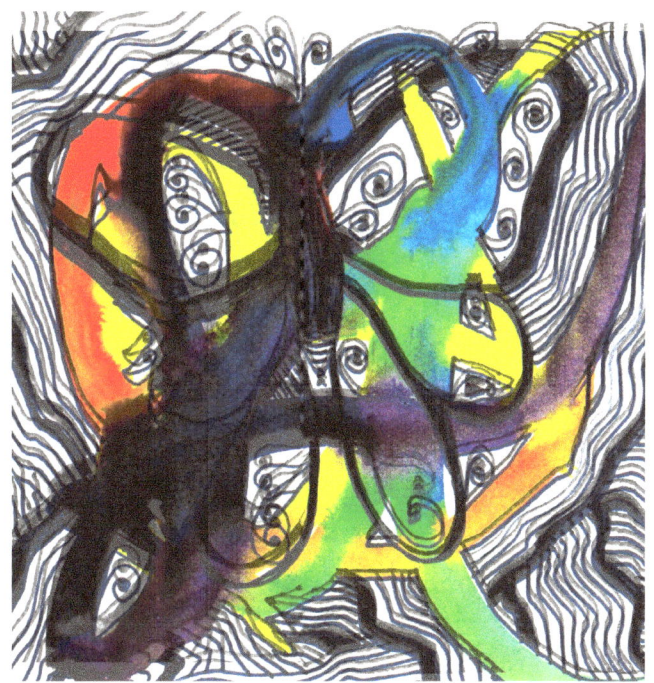

BUTTERFLIES

MIND GAMES

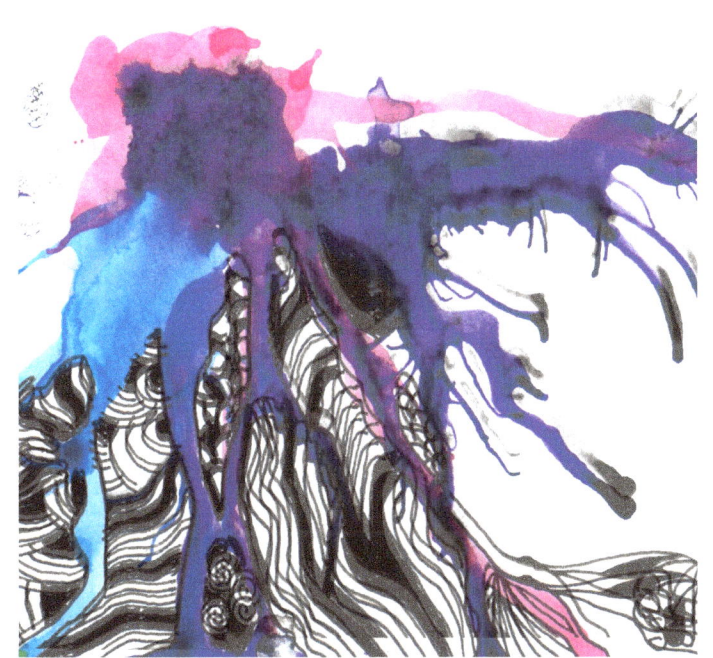

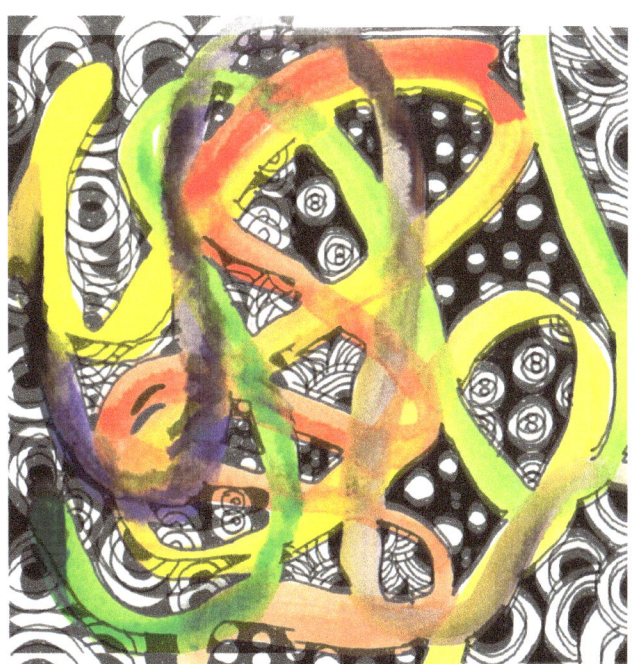

When you find you are blocked by fear, stop, take a breath and reach for the hope that drives you!
-Alisann

ABOUT THE AUTHOR

Alisann is a Fine Artist. She specializes in Dog and Floral Portraits. She has been painting since she was 10 years old. Through her life Alisann worked primarily in acrylics, but in 2019 switched to Oils. It changed her art in a very positive way.

She lives in the Pacific Northwest with her husband, Rick, and their rescue pup Rocke.

Her paintings can be viewed on her website www.artbyalisann.com

She has illustrated 8 Dog themed coloring books for adults—LOVE DOGS

A Myndful Coloring Journal—includes Mandalas and Hamsas

Alisann is a Certified Instructor—The Art of Kumomi™

Alisann Smookler—Artist, Author, Reiki Master, Certified Feng Shui Practitioner

Alisann's coloring books can be found on

Amazon.com (Search—Alisann)

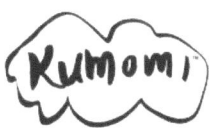

Karen Elaine developed Kumomi™ to enhance the health and well-being of herself and to share with others. She shares this amazing experience throughout the country. www.karenelaine.com

I found many gifts in my journey with cancer.
It has taken me places I did not know I needed to go.
If you face a challenge, be open to the gifts that are waiting for you.
Those gifts are precious.
Namaste'
-Alisann

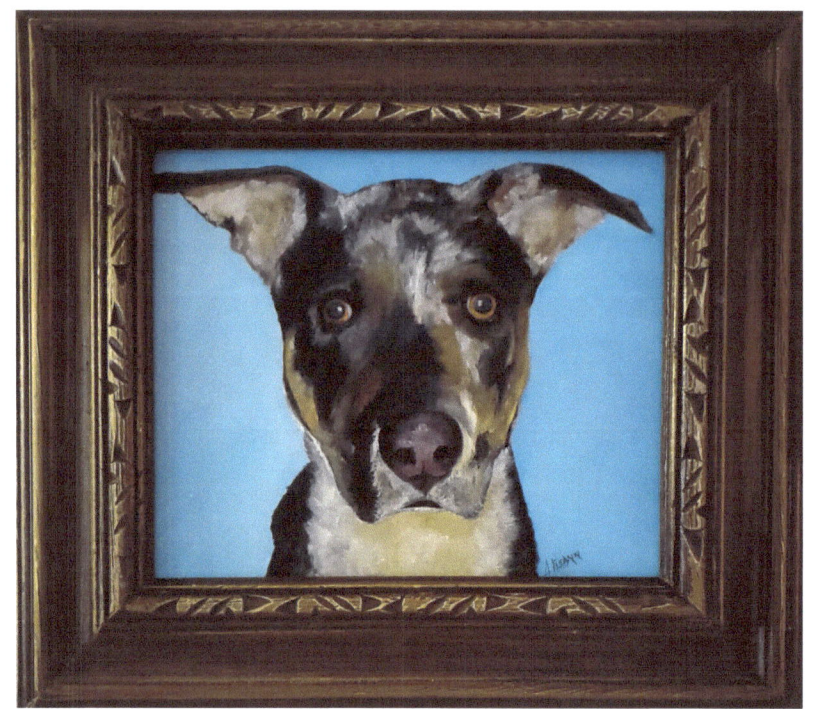

ART BY ALISANN

All Rights Reserved 2023© All of the artwork contained in this book is the sole property of Art by Alisann. No reproductions, in any form, is permitted without the written permission of Art by Alisann.

www.ingramcontent.com/pod-product-compliance
Lightning Source LLC
Chambersburg PA
CBHW051931210526
45473CB00006B/2217